MATTHEW MEAD'S
Backyard Style

FOUNDER, CREATIVE DIRECTOR, EDITOR IN CHIEF
Matthew Mead
MANAGING EDITOR Jennifer Mead
EXECUTIVE EDITOR Linda Bullock
SENIOR EDITOR Sarah Egge
GRAPHIC DESIGNER
Brian Michael Thomas/Our Hero Productions
STUDIO ASSISTANT/DESIGNER Lisa Bisson
CONTRIBUTING GARDEN EDITOR Tovah Martin
CONTRIBUTING PHOTOGRAPHER Helen Norman

Matthew would like to thank everyone involved in this beautiful volume of BACKYARD STYLE, including the team of both Time Inc. Home Entertainment and Oxmoor House. In addition to our feature stories and home owners, I would like to thank Annie Sloan of Annie Sloan Chalk Paint, Brookdale Fruit Farm, Mark Elmore, Sandy and Jim Gorman, Carol Mackay, Tovah Martin, Sally McElroy, Marie and Everett Mead, Helen Norman, John Olson, the Pilato family, Jan and Charlie Preus of the 1750 Inn at Sandwich Center, Lee Repetto, Rosaly's Garden, The Grenon Trading Company, The Kimball-Jenkins Estate, Donna Welch, Mary and Gordon Welch, and Bunny Williams and her team.

OXMOOR HOUSE
VICE PRESIDENT, BRAND PUBLISHING:
Laura Sappington
EDITORIAL DIRECTOR Leah McLaughlin
CREATIVE DIRECTOR Felicity Keane
SENIOR BRAND MANAGER Nina Fleishman Reed
SENIOR EDITOR Erica Sanders-Foege
MANAGING EDITOR Elizabeth Tyler Austin
ASSISTANT MANAGING EDITOR Jeanne de Lathouder

MATTHEW MEAD'S BACKYARD STYLE
EDITOR Meredith Butcher
ART DIRECTOR Christopher Rhoads
PROJECT EDITOR Emily Chappell Connolly
ASSISTANT DESIGNER Allison Sperando Potter
SENIOR PRODUCTION MANAGER Greg A. Amason
PRODUCTION MANAGER Kimberly Marshall
CONTRIBUTING DESIGNER Teresa Cole

PUBLISHER Jim Childs
VICE PRESIDENT, BRAND & DIGITAL STRATEGY
Steven Sandonato
VICE PRESIDENT, FINANCE Vandana Patel
EXECUTIVE DIRECTOR, MARKETING SERVICES
Carol Pittard
EXECUTIVE DIRECTOR, RETAIL & SPECIAL SALES
Tom Mifsud
EXECUTIVE PUBLISHING DIRECTOR Joy Butts
PUBLISHING DIRECTOR Megan Pearlman
DIRECTOR, BOOKAZINE DEVELOPMENT & MARKETING Laura Adam
ASSOCIATE GENERAL COUNSEL Helen Wan

SPECIAL THANKS Katherine Barnet, Jeremy Biloon, Dana Campolattaro, Susan Chodakiewicz, Rose Cirrincione, Jacqueline Fitzgerald, Christine Font, Hillary Hirsch, David Kahn, Mona Li, Amy Mangus, Nina Mistry, Dave Rozzelle, Ricardo Santiago, Adriana Tierno, Vanessa Wu

We welcome your comments and suggestions about Time Home Entertainment Books. Please write to us at: Time Home Entertainment Books, Attention: Book Editors, P.O. Box 11016, Des Moines, IA 50336-1016

If you would like to order any of our hardcover Collector's Edition books, please call us at 1-800-327-6388, Monday through Friday, 7 a.m. to 8 p.m., or Saturday, 7 a.m. to 6 p.m., Central Time.

With any craft project, check product labels to make sure that the materials you use are safe and nontoxic. The instructions in this book are intended to be followed with adult supervision.

NOTE: Neither the publisher nor the author is responsible for your specific health or allergy needs that may require medical supervision, or for any adverse reactions to the recipes contained in this book.

I've always lived in New England,

and with warm months spanning barely half the year, I learned early on to savor them. At my childhood home, our humble backyard was a haven of summertime activities. My parents are resourceful Yankees (pioneers for today's Green movement, I suppose) and they used what they could find to make it special. They recycled railroad ties to create raised garden beds. They salvaged glass and metal tiles from resurfacing projects on Main Street to make a patio. We had a hibachi grill and a red picnic table that my father made. The yard was the place we celebrated birthdays, held family BBQs and whiffle ball games, and ate our fill of picnic sandwiches, ice cream, and hefty slices of watermelon. Some nights we pitched pop tents for sleepovers under the stars with s'mores and sparklers.

My wife and daughters and I have tried to foster memories in our own backyard. We created a getaway feeling with privacy shrubs and even have a place to hang a hammock. There's a patio, a vintage table and chairs, statues, and planters. The birdbaths attract a family of cardinals year after year. Our gas grill—a bit larger than the old hibachi—is in use for as many meals as we can possibly prepare there. Just as when I was a kid, it's a place to gather friends and family, to work in the garden, and to relax in the hammock, watching the white clouds roll by as a neighbor mows his lawn and fills the air with the scent of cut grass.

These pages are all about capturing the inspiration of backyards everywhere. I wanted to share all the ways to live in, savor, decorate, and create your own at-home haven. I've included my very favorite porches, patios, and decks, as well as easy outdoor party ideas featuring delicious food and drinks with seasonal fruits and flowers. Whether your warm-weather season is as fleeting as mine or a yearlong pleasure, there are hundred of ideas here to help you enjoy every moment.

Make some memories!

Facebook.com/matthew.mead.37
Instagram.com/matthewmeadstyle

32

62

94

MATTHEW MEAD'S
Backyard Style

All Decked Out

NOTHING SAYS SUMMER LIKE AN AL FRESCO DECK PARTY THAT'S AS SIMPLE AS IT IS BEAUTIFUL, THANKS TO READY-MADE FOOD AND ICY COCKTAILS.

The sheltered, leafy backyard of Lee Repetto's home in Sandwich, Massachusetts is the setting for a late afternoon repast on a sunny summer day. A jaunty green umbrella provides additional shade for guests.

A quick trip to a local farm stand and Trader Joe's provides Lee with all she needs to whip up an impressive assortment of tasty appetizers, refreshing cocktails, and sweet desserts that can be assembled and made ahead of time—giving Lee the opportunity to relax and enjoy her guests when they arrive.

As a busy shop owner (her store, The Spotted Cod, is a hot spot for local décor enthusiasts and tourists who visit the Cape), Lee Repetto is a firm believer in the importance of getting together with friends to unwind, catch up, and "break bread" when time permits. Impromptu gatherings like this one often turn out to be the most enjoyable for Lee and her friends, but only if she remains true to the motto that you don't have to make everything from scratch in order to eat well. Pull together your own backyard feast (OPPOSITE) by taking a quick trip to a specialty grocery store (Lee is a Trader Joe's fan) to stock up on Italian sodas, deli meats, fresh herbs and cheese, baked bread, even flowers. Lee's signature style is carried out to her backyard sanctuary: A vintage drinking fountain (LEFT) filled with ice is put to use as a place to keep drinks cool—a perfect example of Lee's knack for finding a modern use for vintage buys.

Simple flourishes (BELOW, LEFT TO RIGHT) up the wow factor at even the most casual gatherings. Herb-infused ice cubes, vintage glassware, and natural décor like fern fronds set into old glass bottles are thoughtful touches that bring a touch of elegance to the table.

Backyard Style **11**

Lee's deck is surrounded by 12-foot tall rhododendrons that bring additional privacy to the area. Here, guests can cozy up on cushioned benches and wooden chairs while enjoying the bevy of summer cocktails Lee has on hand. Plump cushions from her shop add a layer of comfort to outdoor furniture and can be brought in each night or stored in weather-proof totes.

An assortment of pretty cotton napkins (RIGHT) is a step up from the usual cook-out paper variety. Fill glass test tubes or cylinders with distilled water and a sprig of lavender (BELOW LEFT) and freeze for a flavorful way to keep drinks cool. Hang outdoor lighting (BELOW RIGHT) from nearby trees, shrubs, or pergolas to extend the party into the evening hours.

Island Whisper Cocktail

This icy cocktail imparts a sweet tropical flavor via pineapple juice, tempered by the acidity of grapefruit juice. Refreshing on a hot summer day, it is garnished with juicy pineapple spears and pineapple mint—a variety that many consider one of the most attractive in the mint family. With its green leaves edged in white, this mint emits a light pineapple scent when its leaves are brushed or touched.

1⅓ cup pineapple juice

1 cup pink grapefruit juice

8 oz good quality gin

Pineapple spears and mint for garnish

1. Fill four glasses with ice; mix the juices and gin together in a glass pitcher and stir well to blend the flavors.

2. Pour equal amounts of the cocktail mixture into each glass and stir. Garnish each with a pineapple spear and a sprig of mint.

3. If making ahead, refrigerate the cocktails and add the ice directly before serving.

Raspberry-Mint Mojito

Herbs and edible flowers have been used for centuries to flavor foods and drinks, and mint is an all-time favorite. This thirst-quenching cocktail boasts the addition of tart-sweet raspberries for an added kick to ignite the taste buds.

1	cup Dragonberry Rum	2	tablespoons simple syrup
24	mint leaves	4	cups chilled club soda
3	limes cut into wedges		Ice
1	cup raspberries		Mint and lime to garnish

1. Gently crush mint with a muddler or the back of a spoon.

2. Squeeze the limes into a glass pitcher and add in the mint. Pour in simple syrup to cover and stir; add in ice.

3. Pour in rum, raspberries, and club soda to taste and stir well. Serve in a glass of your choice and garnish with chopped up lime wedges and a few sprigs of mint.

Berry Citrus Breeze

The simplicity of this cocktail will make it a go-to favorite for a variety of summer gatherings. Using basic bar-stock ingredients, it is an icy beverage that can be created in minutes.

1   shot Dragonberry Rum

1   shot orange liqueur

    Club soda, chilled

    Strawberry for garnish

1. Pour the first two ingredients into a chilled or frozen glass. Stir to blend, and then add in club soda to taste. Stir carefully to avoid removing the carbonation of the soda.

2. Cut a small slit into a plump strawberry and slip it onto the rim of the glass as a garnish.

Tropical Temptation

This piña colada-inspired cocktail will be a hit with guests who love a taste of the tropics. Chill each ingredient well before blending and serve with plenty of ice.

1   liter of coconut water

1   cup pineapple vodka, chilled

1⅕   cups pineapple juice

⅕   cup orange juice

      Fresh pineapple chunks and oranges slices

1. Pour first four ingredients over ice in a tall pitcher. Stir well to blend.

2. Garnish with pineapple chunks and orange slices.

Whether you consider them a vegetable or a fruit, it's a moot point. Everyone, it seems, loves tomatoes, and plucked straight from the vine or tossed in a salad of red and orange cherry tomatoes, fresh corn niblets, and diced red onion, they are a signature sign of summer. (Find Tomato-Corn salad recipe on page 20).

SUMPTUOUS PLATTERS

When temperatures climb, hearty fare is often just too much to digest. Summer meals lend themselves to grazing on appetizers, salads, and savory nibbles that can be assembled and served up in minutes. A crisp baguette is toasted and spread with an herb dip (above, left), then topped with thin slices of ready-to-serve pot roast from Trader Joe's and fresh oregano. Elevate the oh-so-predictable tray of cheese and crackers by switching out a few key elements (above, right): Arrange a goat cheese log on a simple white platter and top it with sliced red grapes and toasted pine nuts. Drizzle it with honey and serve alongside crisp, seeded flat bread and crackers. A crudité platter (left) invites guests to nibble throughout the evening. Miniature zucchini spears, baby carrots, and crackers are served with a creamy edamame dip. Find all recipes on page 20.

A small weathered wheelbarrow moonlights as a charming bar cart holding bottles of wine, fresh lemons, and additional glassware.

Dessert on a hot summer afternoon is a dish best served cold. Lee's friend Peggy Carpenter often brings along her much sought after chocolate cake—a favorite of Lee and her circle of friends—while Lee serves up a simple but tasty blend of tossed peaches and honey. A vanilla-bean cookie from Trader Joe's rounds out the dessert offering. To make the peach salad, combine 6 cups of sliced peaches in a bowl with ½ cup sweet white wine, 2 tablespoons of honey, 2 teaspoons lemon zest, and three sprigs of rosemary. Let the peach mixture macerate in the fridge for several hours. Spoon the peaches into parfait glasses and drizzle with the juice from the bottom of the bowl. (Find chocolate cake recipe at HolidayWithMatthewMead.com).

Tomato and Corn Bread Salad

Take advantage of the best fresh corn and tomatoes of the season to make this zesty, colorful salad.

4	cups fresh corn cut from the cob
¼	cup red onion, coarsely chopped
2	pints of heirloom cherry tomatoes, sliced into quarters
15	pieces French baguette cut into ½-inch slices
½	teaspoon freshly ground pepper
2	teaspoons kosher sea salt
6	tablespoons extra virgin olive oil

In a medium bowl place the corn, onions, and tomatoes. Add in the salt, pepper, and olive oil. Toss well and refrigerate for several hours. Remove from refrigerator and toss with freshly toasted bread slices. Serve immediately.

Cherry tomatoes come in a variety of colors from yellow, pinkish-red, to a deep red. Most are sweet and slurpy.

Edamame Basil Dip

The addition of basil-infused olive oil and toasted pine nuts take a pre-made specialty dip to a whole new gustatory level.

1	container of Trader Joe's edamame hummus
¼	cup toasted pine nuts
	fresh basil
1	teaspoon basil olive oil

1. Toast pine nuts in a skillet until warm and slightly browned

2. Let pine nuts cool and stir them into the hummus.

3. Spoon the hummus into a small, shallow bowl. Make a small divot in the dip and pour the basil oil into the hollow. Garnish with fresh basil.

Steak and Herb Crostini

A warm baguette is layered with a creamy dip and topped with tender slices of beef. Slice it into hors d'oeuvre-sized servings and be prepared to replenish often.

one fresh baguette

pre-cooked deli pot roast from Trader Joe's

Trader Joe's walnut and blue cheese dip

fresh basil

1. Cut baguette in half, length-wise, and place it under the broiler until top is slightly browned and edges are crisp.

2. Remove from oven and spread with the walnut and blue cheese dip. Cut the baguette into individual servings.

3. Top each baguette with a slice of pot roast and garnish with fresh basil leaves.

Herbs on Ice

Summer cocktails taste best served icy-cold. Make your own pretty, flavor-infused ice cubes by slipping in some small berries, lemon zest, and fresh, pesticide-free herbs straight from your garden or the organic aisle of your local grocery store. Not only will they be an extra special garnish for drinks, but will also infuse additional flavor with every sip.

ice cube trays in a variety of shapes and sizes

distilled or boiled, cooled water

fresh herbs, small berries, and/or lemon zest

1. Wash and pat dry sprigs of herbs such as lavender, mint, and lemon thyme and place into each ice cube section.

2. Pour in distilled or boiled, cooled tap water to fill each tray, leaving room for expansion as the ice freezes.

3. Place in freezer for 2-3 hours until the ice is set.

COOL OPTIONS

Scour flea markets and thrift shop for vintage ice trays. Their perfectly square sections create larger, more beautiful cubes than the plastic trays sold today. Alternatively, experiment with silicone trays which come in a variety of shapes and themes including the tubular trays used to make the icy cylinders pictured at right, and opposite.

As the ice melts in the cocktails—or even a simple glass of sparkling water—the herbs and berries release their subtle flavors. Guests will appreciate the extra effort you took to make their drinks special.

Gardener's Eden

GREEN THUMBS HAVE A TENDENCY TO RUN AMOK GATHERING GARDEN PARAPHERNALIA. TO SOLVE YOUR STORAGE WOES, LOOK FOR SECONDHAND CABINETS THAT CAN BE USED OUTDOORS.

Don't have space for a full shed? Slender cabinets like this old school locker store bulky items and weather well. Look for industrial finishes, such as galvanized metal, which won't deteriorate.

BIRDS IN THE GARDEN

McKenny

Look for versatile lockers such as this at flea markets, estate sales, farm sales, and auctions when factories and schools renovate. Doors with ventilation slats allow airflow so potting equipment won't get moldy, and tight-fitting doors keep out water.

Smart storage comes in all shapes and sizes. The trick is to pair right-size containers with items that need a home. Borrowed from a Goldilocks tale, this vintage locker is not too big and not too small. It's just right for garden gear. Made from galvanized metal, it's as weather-hardened as a watering can. Matthew discovered it at a flea market a few years ago and spotted its potential right away. "It probably came from a local school," he says. "There isn't always space for a large yard structure, and this is the perfect size for the weekend gardener."

Vintage books on gardening contain relevant information for today (LEFT). Corral items that need to be handy (BELOW, LEFT TO RIGHT): Leather gloves are durable protection from blisters and thorns. Keep twine for tying up plants in short pots. Placing a short zinc-topped table in the bottom of the locker creates a spot for coiled garden hoses.

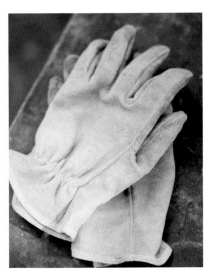

A GARDENER'S FRIENDS

Some of Matthew's favorite implements—both new and old—fill out his backyard cabinet.

1. A well-worn hand rake is perfectly sized to aerate soil around plant bases. Magnets glued to the handle let you stick it where it's easiest to spot. Magnet clips also snag seed packets.

2. Keep soil for container plants in a galvanized pail.

3. Sharp scissors snip both stems and string.

4. Galvanized metal is treated so it won't rust, making it a favorite material for watering cans.

5. Matthew finds vintage books on all kinds of gardening subjects (general guides as well as specific topics) in used bookshops and in bins at flea markets.

6. Metal tags are weather-ready labels for plants and seed rows. Scribe species name and date of planning using permanent markers or a sharp stylus.

7. You can never have enough trowels and hand rakes, so pick up extras that show some wear and tear. You can sand off the rust and repaint handles if needed.

8. Vintage flower frogs are collectible and useful: They hold up heavy blooms in flower arrangements.

9. Look for a variety of pot sizes: Tiny ones are useful to start plants from seed. Medium-size pots are the right size for a kitchen garden of fresh herbs.

Embellish a Planter

To add more personalized function to this vintage storage locker, Matthew added a shelf for short items like twine skeins, flowerpots, and caddies of tools. A combination of magnets and shelf brackets support the shelf and the weight of the items.

- 2 heavy-duty magnets from the hardware store
- 1 piece plexiglass cut to fit the inner dimensions of the cabinet
- 2 vintage metal shelf brackets

  Sheet metal screws

  Level

1. Mark a level line across the back of the cabinet where you want the shelf attached. Affix the magnets to the back of the cabinet equal distance apart, with the top of the magnets at the line.

2. Use sheet metal screws to attach shelf brackets, positioning them along the same level marked line.

3. Insert the plexiglass shelf to rest on the top of the brackets and the top edge of the magnets.

Customizing a metal locker is as simple as using heavy-duty magnets. For a wood cabinet, attach shelf brackets using screws and glue formulated for wood.

To gain sortable cubbies, Matthew stacked weather-ready dividers, such as galvanized buckets and trugs, glass jars, and a divided shelf that once held tools in a hardware store.

BIRDS IN THE GARDEN

McKenny

Sandwich Picnic

JOIN US FOR A PICNIC, WON'T YOU? WE FIND THAT FOOD SIMPLY TASTES BETTER OUTDOORS—ESPECIALLY WHEN YOU PACK THE BASKET WITH INVENTIVE SANDWICHES AND YUMMY SIDES.

Whether you're escaping to a nearby park or setting up an intimate spot under a tree in the backyard, take along interesting sandwiches that feature top-notch ingredients—like this baguette of ham and brie with fig compote.

When Michael packs a picnic basket, he wraps sandwiches in parchment paper using classic butcher's folds, then writes the name in black ink. "It adds to the experience," he says.

For 20 years, Michael Johnston travelled the world for Four Seasons hotels. All the while, he was preparing for his next career. "I always wanted to have a perfect little English cheese shop," he says. Rather than the typical souvenirs, he packed his suitcase with chutneys from India and mustards from France—items he liked and wanted to source in his shop. It seemed inevitable that he would settle in Sandwich, Massachusetts. In 2003, he and husband Steven Cox bought a Main Street fixture, the Brown Jug, which was an antiques shop. Michael reimagined the historic New England building as a specialty gourmet food store. Three years later, after fielding constant requests for prepared food, Michael drew up a soup and sandwich menu, and the picnic business was born. "Regular customers will call and ask for a picnic for four, and say they'll pick it up at noon," Michael says. "I think of the time of year and what the best ingredients would be. I'll gather the linen tea towels, the right wine, and a blanket. It's the perfect Brown Jug lunch." Located a pebble's throw from Cape Cod Bay, the store's carefully packed vintage baskets may head to the shore or simply to someone's front porch. "It makes my skin prickle, I'm so proud," he says. Though it was always a dream, the shop was also a gamble. When he left his hotel career, he had to give up security for the fun of the shop. But the jump was worth it. "Our food is a little different. It's eclectic. It's not the usual everyday thing," he says. "Our own experiences go into the sandwiches."

Growing up in Britain, Michael Johnston always wanted to have an English cheese shop. "I didn't necessarily want to be in England to do that," he says. Global travel helped him source products, such as tarragon mustard from Edmond Fallot in France. His sandwiches (below) showcase these ingredients. Recipes are on pages 41 and 188, and at HolidayWithMatthewMead.com.

PICNIC WITH PANACHE

A packed lunch can be so much more than PB&J and potato chips. **1.** Dried fruits and candy-covered almonds are an energy-boosting snack that won't grow stale. **2.** Chilled water served from a glass or metal vessel tastes bright and fresh. Toss in slices of fruit or cucumbers to make it extra-special. **3.** Pack a blanket to stretch out on, but also include plenty of tea towels, which can perform as napkins and plates in a pinch. **4.** Like dried fruit, pickled vegetables won't spoil, and they offer loads of flavor to brighten any mouthful. **5.** Vintage wood serving utensils are a classier choice than plastic. **6.** Wood trivets are stable bases on uneven ground. Use them to balance drink glasses and carafes of wine. **7.** Bring along plenty of condiments so each picnicker can personalize his or her meal. **8.** Fresh baked oatmeal cookies finish the meal and send you off to naptime.

Earl of Sandwich

"I don't follow trends. I try to create something that I would enjoy, something that represents the ingredients best. I believe that if you always eat the best quality ingredients, you know it will be interesting."
— Michael Johnston

In 1762, John Montagu, the fourth Earl of Sandwich, asked that his meat be put between two slices of bread to make it easier to eat while he played cards.

ROASTED PORK TENDERLOIN

To create this savory sandwich, follow Michael's recipe: He marinates pork tenderloin overnight in green chimichurri sauce, then slow roasts it on the grill. After it's cooked and tender, he carves it and serves pieces on toasted slices of rosemary-flecked focaccia bread with an aged Canadian cheddar cheese, fresh cucumber slices, arugula, and mint leaves cut from his garden. A slather of Greek tzatziki sauce (Greek yogurt, garlic, cucumber, and mint) makes the sandwich moist and delectable.

Information about Michael's other popular sandwiches is on page 188 and at HolidayWithMatthewMead.com

TURKEY AND CRANBERRY

For this popular sandwich, Michael honors New England. He starts with slices of cranberry-pecan loaf from the locally revered Iggy's Bread of the World bakery in Watertown, Massachusetts. Between the slabs, he layers slices of roasted turkey breast, English farmhouse cheddar, and arugula. He makes his own cranberry chutney using Cape Cod cranberries for the final sweet-tangy ingredient. You'll find his chutney recipe on page 188, and at HolidayWithMatthewMead.com.

HAM AND BRIE

For what he calls, "the simplest sandwich ever," Michael relies on the four best components he can source. He cuts a generous portion of a Parisian-style fresh-baked baguette, which is baked locally, and smears the bottom piece with imported fig compote, which is denser than jam. Thickly sliced ham from Nueske's, a meat purveyor in Wisconsin, is the next layer. Michael tops that with creamy fromage de meaux, a Brie-style cheese that has been made in a region outside of Paris in the same manner for centuries.

ROAST BEEF AND HORSERADISH

Michael revisits his English roots with this classic combination. Fresh horseradish root comes from Collinsville, Illinois, the self-proclaimed horseradish capital of the world. He stirs it into some mayonnaise to spread on a rosemary-and-onion focaccia bun. Then he piles on the slow-roasted beef tenderloin. Salty Italian blue cheese is the base, and red onion, lettuce, and tomato are the garden-fresh toppers.

In 1639, Sandwich, Massachusetts, was incorporated and named because its marshes resemble those in Sandwich, England.

Backyard Abode

WHEN BUNNY WILLIAMS BEGAN HER LOVE AFFAIR WITH A
CONNECTICUT HOUSE, SHE DID NOT FIDDLE MUCH WITH THE
FLOORPLAN. BUT THE HOME NEEDED ONE MORE ROOM—OUTDOORS.

The terrace "room" furnishes all the comforts found in the rest of the house and enlisted Bunny Williams' talents as an interior designer. Not only are the boxwoods specifically trimmed low and tight to allow views into the garden beyond, but they appear soft and pillow-like.

Boxwoods in containers (wheeled into the garden over the winter) are the recurring theme.

Blame it on the magnificent 250 year old maple that spreads its august limbs over a generous portion of the backyard—because that is where the idea for an outdoor room first sprouted. Granted, she was outdoors most of the time anyway, but as Bunny realized immediately, "I missed having a terrace." What she wanted was a place where she could lounge with her husband, John Rosselli, and their dogs while sipping something cool and sinking in. The fact that the space has no roof overhead is key, "On beautiful days, you want to be outside under the trees. You want to look at the stars and be one with nature." And when talking about comfort, shade is everything. "If the sun is baking, you're not going to stay outside." Never losing sight of the room's purpose, she also strove to create a clear, unobstructed view of the garden beyond. "I was careful not to confuse the space with clutter, the room is really part of the landscape."

(CLOCKWISE FROM LEFT) Bunny crafted a welcoming entryway courtyard with plenty of places to settle in surrounded by finials on the picket fence to echo the Greek Revival architecture. Elsewhere, jazzier containers cradle coleus and browallia. The covered porch segue features unique Moroccan molding that originally sold Bunny on the house.

MOVING OUT

Not coincidentally, a back door leads conveniently out to a covered porch before opening onto the terrace. Bunny is all about merging, and the covered porch forms a segue between domains. With furniture and art echoing the inside, the porch edges the mood into the wild side while furnishing a place to run from raindrops—and also stash cushions quickly in a downpour.

At Trade Secrets, an annual show that Bunny hosts for charity, she found this faux wicker cast table and paired it with an unused plant pot resulting in ample room to display succulents and coleus. Every year, a bird builds her nest where a candle usually rests in the lantern (OPPOSITE) and a whole lot of twittering ensues. The mirror is meant to reflect the farther garden as well as nearby ferns.

GREEN SCENE

As with all design, creating comfort-space is all about the details and Bunny does it so well by playing nearby nature against distant views of the garden. **1.** Rare succulents are favorites for both Bunny and John, so specimen succulents sit at their elbow. **2.** The goal of the terrace is a clear view of the sunken garden beyond. **3.** Bunny is wild for morning glories so she uses fishing line to give them a leg up. **4.** What's better than reaching over and smelling a scented geranium at your elbow? **5.** Bunny's fascination for faux sculpture drew her to this tole-painted metal fig tree. **6.** Architectural accents can be succulents as well as furniture. **7.** Boxwoods and flowering agapanthus define the space but allow Bunny and John to look beyond. **8.** The sleek lines of a terra cotta urn play counterpoint to the fluffy shrubbery in the garden.

Originally, Bunny had white cushions on the dark Restoration Hardware outdoor furniture. "But those white cushions were all I saw." So she switched shades. Not only is green restive, but it blends in.

THIS PAGE: All of the furniture is strictly functional. Knowing that she would certainly crave something juicy to nibble and a cold drink, the table was integral to the plan. Bunny kept it dark, to echo the other furniture frames. The goal is always to send the focus outward, framing nature at its finest.

OPPOSITE: To keep the furniture from stealing the show, Bunny keeps patterns simple, taking her spectrum from the garden's greenery. "The dogs always want the largest, most comfortable seating," Bunny explains of the double chaise that generally cradles a couple of canines.

Lido Deck

THE ONSET OF SPRING INSPIRES A SIXTY-MINUTE MAKEOVER OF A CHARMING OUTDOOR PATIO AT A SEASIDE NEW ENGLAND INN.

A stack of mismatched transfer plates can be used for casual dining to serve up everything from all-American BLTs to impromptu strawberry shortcake.

A patriotic palette of red, white, and blue serves to unify the varied design elements which were culled from flea markets, tag sales, stores like HomeGoods, and the inn owners' personal décor. Key elements like vintage chairs, a stool, dishware, baskets, and an old watering can and sap buckets were paired with new indoor-outdoor pillows and a cheery red rug.

Matthew met Jan and Charlie Preus, owners of the historic 1750 Inn at Sandwich Center on one of his many trips to Cape Cod, and was enthralled with their second-floor deck overlooking the backyard. Its fun red canvas umbrellas gave Matthew the idea of jazzing up the space for outdoor entertaining with some flea market finds and discount decorating deals. As innkeepers, Jan and Charlie spend much of their time diligently meeting every need of their vacationing guests, so Matthew decided that treating them to a sixty-minute makeover was in tall order. He visited the local flea market The Sandwich Bazaar to gather vintage chairs, tables, and galvanized pieces to use as planters. A local discount design store yielded a colorful woven rug and comfy red pillows. With some quick paint treatments to the furnishings in order to create a unified look—and some plants from a local nursery—the deck is well on its way to being a wonderful outdoor retreat.

A wash of colorful paint to seen-better-days flea market finds and a few simple DIY projects add up to a unified color palette and repurposed design ideas that can withstand the elements with style.

PRETTY ON THE OUTSIDE

When working on an outdoor space, choosing items that will stand up to the elements with style are two of the most important considerations for Matthew. And how each piece works with the others is also key: "When I decorate, no matter what the space, I like to corral all of my finds together to see how they complement each other and see what I need to add," explains Matthew. "The red umbrellas were my inspiration, so I decided to add additional reds and a mix of blues in different shades." Matthew freshened up a flea-market wooden screen (OPPOSITE) with a coat of paint and used it to separate the deck into two zones—dining and relaxation—allowing different guests to use the deck at the same time. A striped linen runner from Matthew's home décor collection (Etsy.Com/Shop/MatthewMeadVintage) adds a pop of color. A metal orb atop a painted vintage stool, and a red watering can and chair are design elements that can be easily rearranged.

THIS PAGE: **1.** Local berries are summer staples that guests of the inn appreciate. **2.** Drinks rest in an old wooden bucket. **3.** An icy drink on the upper deck is popular on a sunny day. **4.** Refills can be stored bug-free inside a lantern. **5.** A tiered, metal thrift store table offers up snacks.

Put old objects to new use: 1. A tempered glass top was added to a painted grain barrel for an instant side table. Fill the base with stones to ensure stability and run a bead of silicone around the rim of the barrel before setting the glass top in place.
2. Cheery striped napkins are tucked inside a bowl.
3. Mismatched blue and white dishes are stacked upright inside an old fryolator basket for easy access when entertaining.

OPPOSITE: Colorful pillows from HomeGoods add a level of comfort to the lounge area of the deck. A rattan chair is the perfect spot for guests to settle into and enjoy a quick refreshment or read a good book. A vintage ashtray stand was given a quick coat of red paint and repurposed as a drink holder.

"Matthew's vision transformed our deck into the perfect oasis—a truly serene and intimate setting."
—Jan Preus

Matthew added a stable top (ABOVE) to a glass bistro table by fitting it with the wooden cover from a damaged pickle crock. He revived it with a fresh coat of white paint and drilled a 2-inch-diameter hole in its center that a patio umbrella can slide through. A vintage rattan and glass vase serves as a cutlery holder and is easily toted from kitchen to deck.

Bucket List

An old wooden ice cream bucket and some galvanized metal sap buckets are given new life with a splash of color—via some red, white, and blue paint and lush, vibrant plants. To prepare metal containers for planting, use a drill and a high-speed steel drill bit to make holes in the bottom, 2 inches apart, and fill the bottom of the containers with 2 inches of pea gravel for optimal drainage.

wooden ice cream bucket

B-I-N Zinsser® white primer

paint brushes

red, white, and blue paint

1. Using a paint brush, prime the surface of the bucket and let dry.

2. Apply a coat of red, white and blue paint to the three divided sections of the bucket.

3. Let dry completely before applying a second coat of each paint color.

4. Use painted buckets as serving containers. Fill them with apples, watermelon, or other grab-and-go snacks.

1

2

3

4

PLANTING INSTRUCTIONS

»   Drill drainage holes in each metal bucket (left) and fill with a layer of pea gravel and soil before adding in heat-tolerant plants of your choice.

»   Mix water-retaining crystals into potting soil before you plant to increase the amount of water held by the container and extend the period between waterings. Ask your local garden center staff which product they recommend.

»   When planting in large containers that you might want to move around, first fill half the container with empty, clean recyclables, such as milk and juice jugs. Then fill in the soil around the jugs. You won't use as much costly potting soil, and the empty jugs don't weigh anything.

Outdoor Escape

FAMED FOR HER PERSONAL GARDEN AS MUCH AS HER INTERIOR DESIGNS, BUNNY WILLIAMS IS DEFINITELY THE OUTDOORSY TYPE. THAT FUSION WAS MOST EVIDENT IN HER POOLHOUSE OUTDOOR ROOM.

Style is pretty much Bunny Williams' middle name. So her spin on Greek Revival (OPPOSITE) includes rustic tree trunk columns with bark left intact and a frieze made of pine cones crowning her temple-like outdoor room. The simple farm table (THIS PAGE) was meant to take the weather in stride. Similarly, all the furnishings were selected to laugh at the elements.

It's a toss up which appealed more to Bunny Williams—the new pool she built or the outdoor room/pool house that it required. An internationally renown interior designer, it was just a hop, skip, and jump to translating the concepts she forged indoors into a fresh air room with all the comforts of home. Siting the structure was a no-brainer—she hiked to the top of the hill on a newly acquired adjacent property, beheld the sweeping view, and knew immediately that she needed a pavilion post haste to admire the scene. Then she did some soul searching and realized that she prefers to sit in the shade after taking a swim and spends the lion's share of spare time reading. So a breezy, open-sided building with a high ceiling was the way to go. Greek Revival is the architectural style echoed all around town, but rustic is the mood in the nearby woodland garden. So she married the two themes magnificently with her accustomed finesse and wit. With plenty of comfy furniture incorporated (including dog beds), this is the place where Bunny, her husband—antiques dealer John Rosselli—and friends come to lounge. Wouldn't you?

Cleverly selected to look like wicker, the vinyl dining chairs (ABOVE, RIGHT) good-naturedly take whatever the weather dishes out. With hurricane lanterns lit, plus a few potted succulents and dahlias to add spark, Bunny instantly has the makings of an impromptu gathering. For its whisper pink flowers that gleam by day and bounce off the candlelight after dark, *Dahlia* **'Café au Lait' is a natural for the mantle (RIGHT).**

OPPOSITE: Knowing that a roaring fire would encourage everyone to linger into the evening and also extend the seasons for the outdoor room, Bunny used a fireplace and mantel as her focal point. Above is a Balinese medallion originally covering a ceiling vent with a wooden stag resting on the mantelpiece as a witty reference to the wilderness in all its untamed glory.

ALL THE COMFORTS

"A bench is fine for perching," says Bunny, "but you need cushions when you really want to stretch out and read."
And that's precisely what Bunny and John do in their outdoor room. Covered with Sunbrella® fabrics selected for their quiet
soothing hues, cushions and pillows take both sun and rain without requiring storage in inclement weather. As a result,
relaxation is easy and requires almost no prep time. Meanwhile, other furniture (especially the faux bois) was chosen
specifically because it is informal, comfy, and echoes the woodland garden nearby.

FLOWER FINESSE

Outdoors or in, no space is complete without flowers in Bunny Williams' book. The designer/author grows her own cutting garden (with an accent on dahlias—her unabashed favorite) and puts those blossoms to work on a regular basis. Dahlia bulbs are started indoors and then transplanted for the longest possible performance duration in New England. Beyond dahlias, other flowers are also infused, giving the outdoor room constantly changing accents for entertaining. But flowers are not just for company. Sometimes, in the midst of summer, all you want to do is loll and dream. What's better than an arrangement to spark both revelries and reveries?

When Bunny Williams arrives in the country, the first order of business is to rally the blossoms in her cutting garden and match them with vases. Although Bunny began her design career under the tutelage of the legendary Sister Parish and Albert Hadley, she never formally studied flower arranging. "I want an arrangement to look impromptu." Glistening shades— like *Dahlia* 'Sherwood's Peach', snapdragons, 'Emerald Tassel' amaranth, and 'Highlander' millet (OPPOSITE)—are a favorite palette.

Making Arrangements

Although Bunny Williams can pull together a massive look-at-me arrangement in the blink of an eye, she leans toward more succinct bouquets for most spaces. Small and tight, these botanical sound bytes do not overpower a room and allow dinner conversation to flow easily back and forth across the table. Toward her goal of making a bouquet appear as if it was just plucked and whipped together in hand, she designs with lightning speed. Often, more time is invested in finding just the right vase to make ingredients such as Zinnia 'Queen Red Lime' (ABOVE, LEFT), Dahlia 'Sherwood's Peach' (BELOW, LEFT) shine together with sea oats and 'Emerald Tassels' amaranth (ABOVE, RIGHT).

1. Not every arrangement needs a "frog" in the base to hold stems steady, but grasses and loose bouquets often do require a foundation. In this case, the squiggly guide wires give further control.

2. In a transparent vase, the foundation should be part of the picture. Fit it in and fill the vase with tepid water.

3. "Many people are afraid to cut their flowers short," Bunny says while fearlessly shearing her stems so the flowers will stand just above the rim line.

4. Bunny begins with a base of sea oats to give the sense of a meadow-in-a-vase, inserting the stems in the holes of the frog.

5. Ornamental grasses require volume to work effectively. To space them evenly and leave room for the flowers, she hooks each blade into the frog's curly wires.

6. Zinnias in greens and whisper pinks (accented by a few more radiant shades tucked in) add "weight" and pop to the bouquet while repeating the meadow motif. The finished understated creation is every inch a Bunny Williams masterpiece.

Summer's Bounty

FIRE UP YOUR TASTE BUDS—GRILLING SEASON IS UPON US! THOUGH YOU CAN BARBECUE THROUGH THE WINTER, SUMMER MARKS THE CONFLUENCE OF GARDEN BOUNTIES AND SUN-WARMED MEALS THAT MAKES GRILLING THE GO-TO CHOICE.

Farm stands and backyard gardens are fertile ground for grilling ingredients. Sweet peppers, tomatoes, corn, and potatoes take on a new dimension when roasted over a hot flame.

Take the stress out of juggling food, sauces, and utensils by setting up a staging area adjacent to the grill. Think of it as the spare area of countertop you use in the kitchen.

Ahhh, there's nothing quite like cooking outdoors—from the ceremony of preparing the grill to the taste of a seared and juicy bite. Whether you belly up to propane-fueled burners on a nightly basis or save stoking the charcoals for special occasions, there are plenty of opportunities to grill as soon as the frost thaws. But grilling tends to be a social occasion. Flavor-infused smoke drifts across yards and draws interested neighbors and hungry friends. Prepare for the crowd by piling up extra ingredients and setting a large table. Everything should be "come and get it" casual, but that doesn't mean it can't also be elegant. With nature as your dining room, choose a picturesque corner to set up a table under a tree or on a spot of soft lawn. Cut blooms or branches to make an easy centerpiece, and layer the table with juice-soaking cloths and napkins.

Wrap up individual silverware settings (RIGHT) so they are easy to grab when the food is ready. Fresh-baked cookies are off-limits to bugs under a cake dome (BELOW, LEFT). Garden twine and snippets of greenery (BELOW, MIDDLE) are unfussy ways to add decoration. Water goblets holding handfuls of cut flowers (BELOW, RIGHT) are bright bouquets that don't take up space.

Grilling Vegetables

There's something about grilling that completely transforms the humble, admirable vegetable into a magical flavor delivery system. Roasting them over a flame brings their juices to the surface and makes their innate sugars ripen and caramelize. Even if you don't think you like vegetables, this preparation method is not to be missed. A simple splash of olive oil and a sprinkling of kosher salt and black pepper is the basic seasoning. To add a second layer of earthy flavor, brush on an olive oil that is infused with garlic, pepper, or another interesting aromatic, then toss the veggies with cut fresh herbs, which will turn delightfully crispy over the flame.

Grill preparation is key to a successful cooking experience: Let the grill warm up on high heat for about 15 minutes. Then scrape the burners clean of the burned bits of leftover food. Finally, oil the rack liberally by brushing on vegetable oil, which will season the rack over time and keep food from sticking.

Leave the vegetables whole, or cut them into sizeable slices and chunks to make handling them easier. For small bites of food, use a grill basket, which will prevent pieces from falling through the rack.

GRILLED ROMAINE HEARTS WITH PARMESAN CHEESE

Did you know you could grill salad? This delicious take on the revered Caesar salad recipe is a cinch to create. Cut whole romaine hearts down the center through the core, so each half has leaves that stay attached. Lay the halves cut-side down on the grill, and heat for up to 5 minutes, until the leaves wilt and start to show grill marks. Remove from the heat and drizzle with your favorite Caesar dressing or vinaigrette, then shave shards of Parmesan cheese on top using a vegetable peeler. The warm leaves will soak up the dressing and slightly melt the cheese.

Sausages are a natural choice for a grilled meal. Choose a variety from the local butcher or meat market, including chicken, pork, veal, and vegetarian. Butter and toast the buns on the grill, and offer several types of toppings and condiments so guests can create their own combination.

Nothing beats a good burger. Start with premium-quality beef with a small amount of marbling: The fat adds moisture and flavor. Stir in a beaten egg yolk (one per pound of beef) to hold the patty together, and a tablespoon of Worcestershire sauce for a savory boost. Matthew's secret method is to form the patty around a dollop of herb butter, which is semi-soft butter stirred with cut fresh herbs. The butter melts inside the burger while it cooks and flavors the meat from the inside out.

Herb Brush

Herb brushes are sure-fire ways to add flavor to any grilled item, both vegetables and meat. As the herbs get warm, their flavor intensifies; as they char, bits break off and stick to the food.

1 **bunch cut herbs, such as chives, thyme, basil, oregano, sage, or rosemary**

1 **skein twine**

3 **wooden spoons**

½ **pound (16 tablespoons) unsalted butter**

salt and pepper, optional

1. Form the herb bunch around the handle of the wooden spoon, and secure with loops of twine. Tie off and trim the ends of the twine.

2. Melt the butter in a small saucepan or heatproof dish over the grill. Stir in salt and pepper to taste, if desired.

3. Dip the ends of the herb brush in the melted butter, and use the brush to baste food as it cooks.

Although they won't char the same way, herb brushes can be used to flavor food cooked indoors as well.

Grilled Peaches and Biscuits

This desert is so delicious and decadent, no one will know it's also quick and easy. The heat from the grill makes the peaches rich, juicy, and sweet.

Ripe peaches, cut in half

Buttermilk biscuits, purchased or fresh baked

Vanilla ice cream

Honey, optional

1. Using tongs, place the peaches cut-side down on a hot grill. Cook for about 5 to10 minutes, until they soften and grill marks appear.

2. Meanwhile, warm the biscuits on the grill in a heatproof pan or on the warming rack.

3. Serve the warm fruit and biscuits immediately with a scoop of ice cream, so the ice cream melts and coats the peaches.

Out on the Porch

THE LIVING IS EASY IN AN ALL-WEATHER SPACE DECORATED WITH COMFORTABLE AND BEAUTIFUL FURNISHINGS FIT FOR ANY ROOM— INDOORS OR OUT.

White columns and shapely balustrades give the add-on porch classic style in keeping with the historic house. They add formality to this outdoor spot, making it perfect for entertaining.

Ellen employs decorating lessons in her outdoor room, creating a focal point with a bamboo sideboard crowned by an ornate gilded mirror. She also places inexpensive Oriental-style area rugs for color and pattern on the wide plank porch floor, which is dark mahogany, a shade similar to the hardwood floors inside.

The July Fourth celebration in antiques dealer Ellen Park's New England town couldn't get much more picturesque. A hometown parade winds along Main Street, right past her and husband George's 1829 Federal style home, which was once a sea captain's house. And she has the perfect perch to enjoy all the festivities—a spacious 10x20-foot porch the couple added when they restored the home nine years ago. "Friends come and have breakfast, and we walk down the driveway to watch the parade," she says. "Then we go back to the porch to finish our bloody Mary's."

The Parks added the porch on the side of the house to replace a small deck. Its proportions were important to Ellen: "I fought for an extra two feet, which meant moving the septic tank, but it was worth it," she says. The square footage allowed her to set up living and dining areas with plenty of elbowroom. For seating, Ellen chose traditional-style wicker with cushions covered in weather-ready fabric.

Ellen didn't make many concessions to the weather, however. She opted to decorate the porch with furniture, rugs, and accessories as she would an indoor room, but with an eye to longevity. "I go to tag sales. It's a little game that I play. If it's going to be an oil painting, it can't be any more than $10," she says. "I try to find bargains because the life expectancy is shorter." In the winter, she brings the art, mirrors, and lamps indoors and covers the furniture, but that's only for a brief period. "This really is like another room in our house for a good part of the year," she says.

Inexpensive accessories, such as framed fruit prints (ABOVE RIGHT), are tag-sale finds. When Ellen and George Park added this porch onto their 1829 home, they chose classic columns and railing spindles to complement the home's look. The chandelier hangs from an old-fashioned beadboard ceiling (RIGHT).

Not everything has to be vintage as long as it has the right look, Ellen says. The rustic clock face came from a consignment store. "It's battery operated," she says with a laugh.

INDOOR-OUTDOOR CONNECTION

Ellen's primary goal in furnishing her porch was to make it feel as luxurious as any room in her home. To that end, she laid a foundation of lounging furniture and spacious seating. Plump pillows, upholstered cushions, and area rugs soften the hard materials of the porch. Table lamps create a glow in the evening and make the space functional for reading or conversation after dark. And finally, accessories add the last layer of comfort. Ellen included framed artwork, informal garden bouquets, and collectibles to brighten the space. Potted annuals (ABOVE) can be changed as the seasons do. To learn how to embellish a plain flower pot like this one with paint and découpage, turn to page 92.

1

2

3

4

DETAILS THAT MATTER

Extra touches make the porch feel and function like an indoor room. It's this layer that elevates the porch from ordinary to truly inviting. **1.** The early-1900s mirror acts as seasonal art by reflecting pretty plantings in the yard. **2.** Flowers are cut from nearby hydrangea bushes and arranged in antique silver vases. **3.** Chairs that have interesting shapes and textures fill blank corners and can also be pulled into use for a crowd. **4.** The vintage chandelier requires no wiring, so Ellen can pack it away in the winter months. **5.** A peek through the railing offers a glimpse of waiting snacks and a place to recline. **6.** A stack of platters and trays is handy for beverage or meal service. **7.** Lamps and candles cast intimate light and make the space useful at night. **8.** Ellen places decorative items atop the sideboard just as she does in her dining room.

5

6

7

8

To keep the space from feeling one-note, Ellen mixed new and old furnishings, added an abundance of different-color pillows and cushions, and varied the texture and color of the wicker pieces.

Butterfly Planter

Personalize an off-the-rack planter from the home center with paint and botanical art.

- **1** plastic flower planter with a concrete look

- **1** quart latex paint

- **1** 2-inch paintbrush

- **1** 1-inch paintbrush

- **1** paint pen in metallic gold

- **1** book of nature

1. Make a color-photocopy of a chosen image from the book. You may have to reduce or enlarge the image to make it fit the space on the planter.

2. Brush latex paint all over the planter and let dry.

3. Using a clean paintbrush, apply ModPodge® to the area when you want to stick on the motif. Press the motif into the glue, then brush more over the surface of the paper to create a seal. It will dry clear. Finally, use the gold paint pen to highlight any details on the planter or around the motif.

Use this same technique on small flowerpots or large window boxes. You can add monograms, house numbers, or any motif of your choosing.

Fill the planter with soil and flowers, or pack it full of ice to chill beverages. Once dry, the découpage glue seals the image and protects it from dripping water.

Night Lights

AN EVENING OUTSIDE CALLS FOR JUST THE
RIGHT ILLUMINATION AND THE RESULTANT GLOW
IMPARTS A MAGICAL AMBIANCE TO ANY SETTING.

An assortment of colored glasses—collected at tag sales in shades of purple and amber—become flickering beacons on a patio table, set for entertaining guests.

Grab some medium-sized fairy lights and a sturdy ladder and wrap them around the frame of a wooden pergola to bring it to life. Christmas lights can be used out of season to cast just enough glow to ensure uninterrupted star gazing.

The beauty of a summer's evening is that it can seemingly go on forever, especially if you incorporate some subtle elements that will extend the light beyond sundown. Candles in all shapes and sizes (some with citronella to ward off biting insects) can be placed in glasses, bottles, or storage jars. It's no secret that everything looks better bathed in warm light, and you can set an entire scene for a very small investment. Use inexpensive strands of Christmas lights to illuminate the edge of a shed or outbuilding or add light strings to leafy trees for spectacular diffused lighting. Comfy chairs and pillows (LEFT) set the scene for evening conversation. Plan a meal outside just as twilight approaches or set out simple snacks. And the sparkly light infusions are like having an ultra-fun party host: the warmth, flickering shadows, and subtle nuances given off by their light will make guests feel as though they are somewhere special.

A deep purple parfait glass (BELOW, LEFT) strikes a regal note despite having been plucked from a flea market vendor for pennies on the dollar. Glass floral stones reflect the light from miniature battery-operated strand lights nestled in a glass bowl (BELOW, RIGHT).

Floating sunflowers are hollowed in the very center to fit a wax tea light. This arrangement works well as a centerpiece for both the dining and coffee table. Simply fill a large mixing or salad bowl with water and float sunflowers which have been cut where the stem meets the bloom. Keep the bowl filled with water to keep the fresh blooms hydrated for several days.

FLICKERING GLOW

Candles, candles everywhere: **1.** A pewter platter holds a mix of pillar candles. Arrange them at the table and surround the base with fresh leaves. **2.** A wire cloche corrals a trio of decorative candles on a metal base. The wire form allows air to flow freely and offers an interesting focal point. **3.** A terracotta bird feeder doubles as a hanging lantern with the addition of a few votive candles. **4.** Metal utility light-bulb protectors have a trendy recycled vibe when placed over colorful pillars.

CANDLE POWER

One of the most inexpensive ways to set the mood for entertaining is candlelight. **1.** Wrap or wire light strings to trees and outbuildings and use extension cords to reach a nearby outlet. **2.** Illuminate flower arrangements with micro light branches that keep centerpieces in focus even as night falls. **3.** Ensure that seating is comfortable with soft cushions so that guests will linger on to star gaze once darkness sets in. **4.** An antique glass storage jar is tied with twine and secured to a hanging plant holder for an instant lantern. **5.** A colored glass votive with a pinecone candle tucked inside adds whimsy. **6.** While candles add a layer of enchantment, they should never be left unattended and should be fully extinguished before every guest "turns in." **7.** Votives flicker in the night. **8.** Protect vintage rattan furniture with a protective coat of clear shellac.

A brown, glass decorative bottle is wrapped in a criss-cross pattern of miniature battery-operated light strands to create a luminous sculpture. Tiny pieces of black electrical tape hold the light strings in place.

Sunflower Votive

The vibrant color of showy sunflowers makes for a scene-stealing centerpiece. Add sparkle by hollowing out their centers and inserting a simple tea light. Float several in a bowl for no-fuss presentation and care and place in the center of an outdoor table lined with lit votives.

Sunflower blooms with the stem removed

A grapefruit spoon and small, sharp knife

Wax tea lights

Wooden or glass salad bowl

1. Using a sharp knife make a slit in the center of each sunflower and use a grapefruit spoon to hollow out the center.

2. Insert a small tea light into the hollowed out space.

3. Fill a salad bowl with water and set the flower votives in and light. Do not leave lit candles unattended.

Place several sunflower-filled bowls along the length of an outdoor table to make a colorful statement.

Sunny Centerpiece

Create a living light show with a bouquet of sunflowers and several electric branches. Fill a sturdy glass vase with sunflowers and water and place inside a tall, woven basket. Arrange the lighted stems between the outside of the glass vase and the inner edge of the basket, ensuring the branches do not come in contact with the water in the vase.

Hydrangeas

A CAPE COD GARDENER AND FLORIST SURROUNDS HER HOME WITH COLORFUL SEASIDE HYDRANGEAS THAT BLOOM FROM HER GARDEN.

Bountiful profusions of hydrangea billow from the perimeter of the house in a way that looks natural and unplanned, creating a colorful frame for the charming Cape Cod cottage of Carol Mackay.

A mid-century iron settee and its matching chairs and side tables add up to an inviting place for Carol to sit back and enjoy her garden and the heavenly aroma wafting from the many hydrangea bushes nearby. For Carol, it is the perfect place for family gatherings, quiet reading, bird-watching, or hosting friends for cocktails. Covered in a complementary linen-look fabric, the settee cushions blend in with the wall of lilac and purple blossoms that surround the space.

Carol Mackay is a botanical master who has designed her back yard and favorite blooms with the skill of the best flower arranger. While her canvas is large, it is just an extension of her work as a wedding and special occasions florist. Here at her home she moves beyond the flower basket and instead edges her house, patio, and gardens with colorful blooms. Carol's style is simple and fresh, thus inspiring the name of her business, Seaside Simplicity. Her garden is a study of that sensibility with shapely but subtle statuary, myriad hydrangea varieties, and a mix of garden blooms that seem as though they are destined to be together.

Carol's love of arranging extends beyond her magnificent yard and jaw-dropping floral arrangements to sculptural displays such as this wire basket filled with sea fans, shells, and weathered driftwood that Carol has collected over time from the many beaches near her home. The colors of each natural element echo the color palette of her garden.

FULL CIRCLE

Pluck the individual blooms off a large blossom and float them in a vintage dish filled with water (LEFT) for a refreshing floral display. A pergola (BELOW) constructed of items from the home center is painted a subtle blue-gray to blend in with the surrounding hues. A vintage cloth hung on one side creates an instant picnic area that has been layered with grass mats, pillows, and bamboo stools.

"I designed my garden so that year-round I can find something colorful, textural, and interesting to make into an arrangement." –Carol Mackay

A hydrangea bush, resplendent with lush blooms, hugs a stately cement garden bench—leaving just enough room to sit or use as a place to assemble freshly cut flowers into bouquets. To ensure bountiful blooms, the hydrangea plant requires plenty of water and pruning. So don't be afraid to cut the blossoms.

Hydrangea Wreath

Create your own beautiful hydrangea wreath with cut blooms from your yard or local florist.

1   **9-inch oasis foam wreath**

1   **dozen freshly cut blue hydrangea cuttings**

24   **large hydrangea leaf clusters or salal leaves**

1. Soak the oasis wreath in water for 30 minutes. Remove from water and place on a flat work surface. Begin by placing the leaves around the outer edge of the wreath form.

2. Continue with the center of the wreath and then the inner circle. The wreath should look sparse, with ample gaps and foam still showing.

3. Break large mop-head blooms into palm-sized clusters. Leave plenty of stem on the bloom to insert firmly into the wreath.

4. Add flowers to the wreath, making sure the blooms remain uniform in size, and then evenly fill in the gaps.

5. Hang out of direct sunlight or lay flat on the table as a floral centerpiece.

6. Use a spray water bottle to spritz the wreath daily.

Hang a fresh wreath on your door to greet visitors, or place in the middle of a table and nestle a glass hurricane—bearing a candle—in the center of the wreath.

Blooming Cake Stand

A cake stand blossoms with pretty petals for a simple-to-make dessert serving piece.

Glass cake stand

Mod Podge®

Small paint brushes

Photocopied images of hydrangea blossoms

1. Turn hydrangea blossoms into everlasting blooms by placing single blossoms on your copy machine to make paper flowers.

2. For the cake stand, use a small paint brush to apply Mod Podge® to the paper flowers.

3. Adhere the paper blooms to the underside of the stand. Wipe the top surface clean with window cleaner. Do not submerge the stand in water.

Dress up glass or ceramic coasters (ABOVE) with more of the paper flowers. Adhere them to the top of each coaster with Mod Podge® and brush with clear matte acrylic sealer.

Glassware can be easily embellished by color-copying and gluing on images of your favorite blooms. If you don't have access to a copier, use floral images from old books or magazines.

Backyard Pizza

WHAT'S THE SUREFIRE LURE TO ENTICE YOUR FAMILY OUTDOORS?
BAKE UP A SAVORY, FRESH-MADE PIE AND WATCH THEM FLOCK.

Want the ultimate backyard pizza? Fire up a wood burning brick oven like this masterpiece at In Situ and you've got the Rolls Royce. Not only will your pizza bake almost instantly in a couple of minutes, but that pie will be the most savory flat bread you've ever tasted. Talk about a crowd pleaser!

For the Pilato family, stone is a way of life. By the time Mike (far left) and Sal Pilato (far right) were growing up, most Italian families had their own brick ovens. But prior to WWII, villages used communal wood-fired ovens where families would come to bake their bread and pizza. Raised on freshly baked pizza, Mike and Sal Pilato will tell you—there is no comparison.

Mike Pilato started mixing cement for his father, Pasquale Pilato—master oven builder—in Italy at six years old and he was wielding stone not long after. What did he miss most when he came to the United States in 1972? "The Italian pizza," he says. So when Richard Hartlage asked the Pilatos to build an outdoor wood-burning oven into the plan for the gardens he designed at In Situ, an 8-acre retreat in rural Connecticut, they knew exactly how to configure the dome-shaped oven. And they could scarcely wait for the test run. Built with fieldstone from the property but lined with fire bricks (stone alone will not tolerate the searing temperatures) a wood-fired oven uses kindling to slowly build up 700-degree temperatures over a few hours. After that, the bricks hold the heat while the pizzas are shoveled in and out rapid-fire. Baking time takes only two to three minutes, but the full-flavored instant gratification is memorably mouth-watering.

From left to right are stonemasons Mike, Billy, Pasquale, and Sal Pilato (ABOVE RIGHT). Mike's son, also Pasquale, is not shown. Experienced in all things stone, they lined the wood-fired oven with fire bricks (RIGHT).

Family and friends will linger longer outdoors when the pizzas keep coming, especially if you let everyone custom-design their own personal comfort food version. Add some sparkling wine and you've got an impromptu party. The succulent container centerpiece (crafted of hens & chickens in this case) is a constant no-maintenance accent adding punch to your dining area.

COOKING AND LOUNGING OUTDOORS

Look around, and it could be Tuscany. But In Situ sits squarely in Connecticut. Enlisting the rolling countryside to best advantage, landscape architect Richard Hartlage of Land Morphology created the sort of venue that draws the family to remain loitering outdoors. His secret ingredient for extending the call-to-the-wild after sunset? The oven and fireplace that share a mutual chimney keep everyone comfy, cozy, and catered to. Not only is the seating area thoughtfully staged with oversized, teak chairs to sink into, but low walls partition the outdoor kitchen into its own room. Granite tops double as counter space (especially convenient for rolling out pizza), and the floorplan offers other amenities as well. Beyond the oven, Richard feels that the refrigerator is the "make or break" feature. "Anyone who seriously entertains wants to stock a refrigerator full of ingredients to eliminate mad dashes indoors."

With eight acres of gardens farther afield as a backdrop, the outdoor room needed to be oversized to make a statement—and its 15x25-foot footprint is the magic proportion to fit several tables and lots of seating possibilities, including a granite stool carved by Pasquale Pilato.

There's no reason why an outdoor room shouldn't be furnished with furniture that relates to the surroundings while encouraging you to sink in and stay. Made of teak, Richard selected sturdy furniture that would not be tossed around in any weather. Nearby, low-maintenance *Begonia* Dragon Wing™ Red sits on the wall.

1. The tall, capped chimney is critical to provide sufficient draw. 2. Nature repeats motifs in the wild and an outdoor room should follow suit. Not only does the upholstery match, but Richard echoes plant textures with multiple containers of succulents. 3. Beyond the entertaining terrace, the garden moves uphill to the pool with ornamental grasses softening the stone steps constructed by the Pilato family. 4. Hydrangea 'Limelight' is reliable to perform throughout the summer. 5. For the nearby pool house, the Pilatos built tall stone pillars to shoulder the wisteria climbing on a recycled pine arbor. 6. Quickly assembled cheese, tomato, and olive pizza is served straight from the pizza oven. 7. Extra arugula or baby spinach not used on pizzas can be tossed into a quick salad. 8. Delight everyone with a dessert pizza. Crisp a crust, allow it to cool, and spread with nutella and a freckling of fresh raspberries.

Baking in the Brick Oven

Whether you go for the crème-de-la-crème wood-fired oven or select a gas-powered version, pizza prep is the same and the results are like nothing else you've ever popped into your mouth.

1. Start with fresh dough or par-baked crust from the grocery store, both flat-bread and pre-baked Naan crusts work equally well.

2. Prepare the dough and spread the crust with sauce, then add cheese, fresh tomatoes and olives. When you place toppings less than an inch apart, each slice packs maximum flavor.

3. Add fresh basil leaves before going into the oven. Other fresh herbs can be added as well—traditional favorites include marjoram, oregano, thyme, and rosemary.

4. Once the hot pie is removed from the oven, let it cool slightly for two or three minutes to allow the cheese to firm.

5. Top with more fresh herbs for zesty flavor.

6. Cut into slices with a pizza cutter and move out of the way while hungry guests descend.

Pizza on the Grill

Your backyard grill can become a pizza-producing stand-in, all you need is dough plus your favorite ingredients.

Our lip-smacking grilled pizza was made with salami, olives, cheddar, and mozzarella and then sprinkled with confetti of fresh oregano

1. Prepare the dough, clean the grill, and then spread the pre-heated charcoal evenly below.

2. While the closed grill pre-heats for 10-15 minutes, stretch the dough. Brushing it lightly with olive oil prevents sticking on the grate.

3. Cook for 3-4 minutes and then remove the dough from the grill to receive the topping on the already-grilled side. Sausages and vegetables can be pre-grilled for added flavor.

4. Build your topping and then return the pizza to the grill, close the lid and cook for another 3-4 minutes.

5. Remove the pizza and sprinkle fresh herbs over the top according to your taste.

6. Allow the pizza to cool before cutting and serving.

FRESH HERBS

Whenever you add fresh herbs to a recipe, it ratchets the taste experience up a notch or more. There is no comparison for fresh herbs on a pizza—they add a zesty element. For maximum flavor, sprinkle fresh herbs after cooking. And remember, a little goes a long way with fresh herbs—they will be much more pungent than their dried counterparts. If you really want to have fun, grow them beside your grill or oven to pluck according to whim.

No outdoor oven?
No problem.

Substitute a grill instead.

Easy Rose Garden

WITH THEIR HEAVENLY FRAGRANCE, ROMANTIC ROSES ARE EASY TO LOVE—IT'S THE GROWING OF THEM THAT CAN SEEM SCARY. BUT, BY CHOOSING THE RIGHT VARIETIES AND FOLLOWING OUR CARE TIPS, YOU'LL ENJOY THESE STELLAR BEAUTIES IN YOUR GARDEN AND HOME.

Author Charles Rowan Beye wanted a hobby for his retirement, so he planted this garden. It features heirloom roses of all colors and varieties, such as the yellow Julia Child, the pink Lillian Austin, and the dark pink Gertrude Jekyll (OPPOSITE). "The garden is really my refuge," he says.

Sterling silver, silverplate, and mercury glass vessels have an aged appearance that complements the old-fashioned quality of roses. Here, the blooms are sorted by color into vessels, then similar peach and pink shades are clustered together for an arresting centerpiece arrangement.

With a cup of coffee in hand, Charles Rowan Beye chooses a spot each morning in his backyard garden to sit and sip and take in the early beauty. "I sit there for an hour, meditating, staring at the fountain, and enjoying the peace of the flowers," he says.

In 1999, he and husband Richard placed terrazzo pathways around the yard of their newly purchased Boston-area house. They built raised beds and a pergola. Charlie planted heirloom roses chosen for vibrant color and fragrance. "Then I watered and watered and watered," he said.

Years later and now 83, Charlie says the plants are well established. He cares for them with a rose food applied three times a year, he adds a spore to the soil to combat Japanese beetles, and he continues to water—about a bucket full a week per plant. But the reward for the effort is worth it, he says. "You can't start thinking about how much work it is, or you don't enjoy the time on the bench. You have to imagine you have a full-time gardener waiting in the back," he says with a laugh. "I owe my serenity to the beauty of the garden. I feel very lucky to have it."

A thornless Zephirine Drouhin rose climbs Charlie's fence (LEFT). One of the fountains Charlie has incorporated in his garden sits idle for birds to use as a bath and water source. A cut Lillian Austin bloom also liked its hydration. (BELOW).

ROSE TIPS

CHOOSING — Many of Charlie's roses are the David Austin brand (DavidAustinRoses.com). The English rose breeder who also sells through nurseries in the U.S. cultivates multi-petal varieties prized for their alluring fragrances. They also "repeat," or bloom, all summer.

PLANTING — Pick a spot that gets at least 6 hours of sunlight each day, and work plenty of compost into the soil.

WATERING — If there isn't adequate rainfall, give each plant a gallon-size bucket of water each week.

FEEDING — Charlie recommends the granular version of Bayer Advanced All-In-One Rose & Flower Care, which he applies on a strict schedule, according to package directions, on May 1, June 15, and August 1.

When Charlie planted his garden, visions of the lush formal beds of his childhood home in Iowa danced in his head. "I don't care for the wild style of garden. I like things in boxes," he says. Above all, he wanted the garden to be full of color year-round. "I wanted something in bloom from May to October," he says. "The roses start in June. They're wonderful because they come in waves and go on and on."

As each bush peaks, Charlie might enjoy 30 to 40 blooms, such as on this apricot Westerland climbing bush (ABOVE LEFT), which he'll enjoy from one of the rockers on the porch. He'll snip a mixture of colors and varieties (LEFT) for big dining-table bouquets. Just two blooms form a charming tussie-mussie in a linen sack (ABOVE).

Petals left to dry on a rack can be used for potpourri, food garnishes, or rose water. Find out how to make it on page 137.

Since ancient
times, rose water
has been prized
as a moisturizer,
perfume, and
culinary ingredient.

ROSE WATER IN FOOD

Rose water, which is distilled using steam, carries the subtle aroma of the flowers, and it is used frequently in dishes in North Africa and the Middle East. Early bakers in Europe and the United States used it before vanilla was common. Today, it's a trendy ingredient in cupcakes and martinis, and it can enhance both savory and sweet dishes. It complements many fruits, such as in these mini pies (ABOVE). You'll find the recipe on page 189 and at HolidayWithMatthewMead.com. Make up a batch of rose water using our recipe on page 137 and any variety of rose that you choose. We like the Zephirine Drouhin rose (LEFT), which, like all roses, has edible pink petals. Properly stored in the refrigerator, a bottle of rose water will keep for up to two weeks. A tablespoon of vodka added to the bottle acts as a preservative, so the mixture will last longer.

Rose petals are edible and make lovely garnishes atop this rose-water spritzer (see recipe on page 188 or at HolidayWithMatthewMead.com). But only eat the petals of the flower after washing it. Don't eat flowers that you didn't grow, and don't eat the petals of a plant that has been sprayed with fertilizer or insecticide.

Add a few drops of rose water to your favorite ice cream recipe, or follow our recipe on page 189 and at HolidayWithMatthewMead.com. A garnish of rose flower will provide a hint to the flavor.

When cutting roses, Charlie wears thick garden gloves to protect his skin from thorns. Once inside, he snips the stem ends again under running water at the sink, which helps the flowers hydrate. With fresh water in the vase each day, the blooms will last a week or more.

Making Your Own Rose Water

As it has been done for centuries, this process involves distilling rose vapor into rose water. As the petal-filled water heats and melts the ice on the lid, condensation forms on the bottom of the lid and drips into the empty bowl. When Matthew and Jenny prepared this batch, it took about 3 hours. Three batches made about 1½ cups of liquid, or enough to fill the jar on page 132.

1   Dutch oven or saucepan with a flat, lipped lid

2   small bowls, one to use as the stand and one to catch the drips

2   cups rose petals

3   cups ice cubes

4–8   cups of water, depending on size of pot

1. Place pan on a burner over low heat.

2. Place a small heatproof bowl upside down in the bottom of the pan, then fill the pan with water almost to the top edge of the bowl bottom.

3. Sprinkle in rose petals.

4. Place a heatproof bowl on top of the inverted one. Turn the heat to high to bring the mixture to a boil, the lower the temperature to simmer.

5. Fill the pan lid with ice cubes, and then place the lid on the pan. (If you don't have a lid with a lipped lid, you can use a stainless steel bowl that is large enough to seal the top of the pan.) Simmer for 3 to 4 hours, replacing ice as it melts.

Cherries Jubilee

THE PEAK OF THE SEASON FOR THESE RUBY JEWELS COMES AND
GOES ALL TOO QUICKLY. GRAB A BASKET AND HEAD TO THE NEAREST
ORCHARD OR FARM STAND, THEN TREAT YOUR FAMILY TO THESE
TASTY EATS.

A warm-from-the-oven biscuit is simply a conveyor for fresh cherry jam. Pick any mode of transport for this syrupy confection, including toast, croissants, or buttery scones.

There are 87 calories in 8 ounces of fresh pitted cherries, so a café au lait bowl filled to the rim (OPPOSITE) is a healthy way to get fiber, vitamin C, and potassium into your diet.

One weekend in early June, Matthew and Jenny can be found with many of their neighbors and friends at Brookdale Fruit Farm in Hollis, New Hampshire. It's cherry-picking season in New England, and it doesn't last long. By Independence Day, the fruit will be gone. Matthew and Jenny head out after an early breakfast to beat the sun and heat. With practiced ease, they reach up into the drooping, fruit-laden branches and pluck the stems of the stone fruits, careful to twist gently and not harm the fruit buds of next year's crop. Their thumbs and forefingers (the tools of the job) get stained deep crimson as the morning wears on, but it's a small price to pay for the cardboard box brimming with bright, shiny cherries. "Picking cherries is one of the best ways to engage in the season," Matthew says. He and Jenny will eat much of their bounty straight from the stem, but they also cook them into jam, stir them into batters, and even use them to flavor festive drinks. For a little while at least, it's all things cherry in the Mead house.

Cherries are a stone fruit, like peaches and apricots, and have hard pits. They grow in clusters on branches and come in many colors including pink, orange, and near-black, depending on the variety. Check the schedule at your local orchard because the fruits ripen at different times across the country.

Dark brown sugar and tapioca combine in the filling of this rich and saucy pie. The crust is woven into a lattice pattern to allow the vivid deep cherry color to show through. Serve it with a dollop of freshly whipped cream. The recipe for this pie, and all the foods on these pages, can be found on page 189.

PRESERVING SEASONAL FOOD

Fresh cherries are best when you eat them picked straight from the tree in the orchard, but there are many ways to stretch the enjoyment by preserving them in cherry jam, baking them into pies, or whipping up no-bake desserts like the ice cream or torte on the following pages. These mini tarts (BELOW) are easy enough for kids to make. You'll find the recipe on page 189. To freeze fresh cherries for use later in the year, remove the stems but keep the cherries whole with pits intact. Spread the cherries in one layer on a sheet pan that fits in and sits level in your freezer. Let them freeze hard for a day or up to two days, then slide them off the pan and into a resealable plastic freezer bag. When you want to enjoy them again, pick a few out of the bag, and let them thaw on the counter or in the refrigerator.

Muddle a bunch of fresh cherries to give a batch of margaritas a zing of flavor and bright color. Freeze whole cherries for several hours, and use them in place of ice cubes to keep this drink—or any summertime sipper—cold.

Who doesn't love cherries and chocolate together? Churn the classic combination into cherry-chocolate chunk ice cream using the recipe on page 190. Or, for a quick treat, let store-bought vanilla ice cream soften for 30 minutes, then stir in the cherries, chocolate chunks, and a splash of cherry juice, before re-freezing.

Cherry Torte

Beat the heat with our no-bake cherry torte. Embellish a pre-made spongecake tart shell with orange juice, vanilla custard, and fresh cherries, then top it with a cherry glaze.

1   **12-inch spongecake tart shell from the grocery store or bakery**

¼   **cup orange juice**

8   **ounces cream cheese, room temperature**

2   **cups milk**

1   **3.4-ounce package instant vanilla pudding**

3   **cups (approximate) fresh pitted cherries**

1   **cup cherry jam, homemade or premade**

1   **tablespoon Kirsh**

1. In a medium mixing bowl, beat the cream cheese with an electric mixer until it is very soft. Slowly beat in ½ cup of the milk and stir until it is very smooth. Add the remaining milk and the pudding mix. Beat slowly for 1 minute. Place in refrigerator for 20 minutes until the mixture is thick. Gather all the remaining ingredients.

2. Using a pastry brush, paint the inside of the spongecake tart shell with orange juice until the cake becomes dense and moist.

3. Spoon the cream cheese mixture over the prepared spongecake tart shell and spread it to the edge.

4. Place the cherries over the pudding mixture, completely covering the tart.

5. In a small saucepan over medium heat, cook the jam until it becomes a thick liquid. Stir in the kirsch. Using a pastry brush or spoon, baste the top of the tart with the warm jam mixture. Let cool.

No one will know how simple this no-bake cherry torte is to prepare. Serve it on a cake pedestal to make it special, and garnish with fresh cherry leaves for non-edible decoration.

Backyard Blooms

CREATE A SIMPLE CUTTING GARDEN WITH YOUR FAVORITE
FLOWERING ANNUALS TO PROVIDE YOU WITH PRETTY BOUQUETS
ALL SUMMER LONG.

Rows of zinnias, planted in straight and even lines, bloom in colorful profusions (OPPOSITE). A mix of salvia, cosmos, and scabiosa is a burst of color in a humble kitchen water glass (BELOW).

Arrangements are fun to create and you can place them in a variety of objects you have around the house. Gather a bunch of mismatched vessels from the flea market like bowls, pitchers, and baskets and use them as versatile vases for all types of blooms.

For an easy way to garden, approach the care and nurturing of flowering plants much like you would a vegetable crop. Select flowering annuals that will produce an abundance of blooms like the popular cultivar of zinnias called Cut And Come Again (BELOW), which is a reference to the fact that the more times you cut this blossom, the more blooms the plant will produce. To create a lush garden faster, purchase somewhat mature plants at a nursery and put them in the ground as soon as possible. By mid-July, you will have plenty of flowers to fill your own vases and decorate all the rooms in your home. Many varieties grow well in rows, and with adequate hydration via a sprinkler, hose, or watering wand, a neatly organized patch of blooming flowers is relatively easy to take care of.

A gathering of small vessels mean you can make simple, fool-proof arrangements to adorn side tables inside or out. Yellow coneflowers, cosmos, zinnias, and asters (LEFT, TOP TO BOTTOM) are just a few of the easy-to-find, old-fashioned flowers that grow and propagate easily in the warm weather. For blooms with heavier heads like asters, purchase delicate floral support grids that attach to ground stakes and help keep the heads from breaking in the wind or rain.

Flower bouquets can be as simple or elaborate as you like. For beginners seeking professional-looking results, try grouping blooms by color. 1. A vintage chintz-ware pitcher holds a demure blue and lavender arrangement of bachelor buttons, blue scabiosa, and ageratum. 2. Some centerpieces make a stylish statement when combined in subtle shades of white and green, like this outdoor dinnertime centerpiece of hydrangeas, cosmos, and white zinnia. 3. A vintage hand-woven basket is lined with a glass bottle, filled with tall spiky delphinium and purple stattice, and hung from the finial of an outdoor garden chair.

A mix of old fashioned blooms (OPPOSITE) that you can grow or buy in bundles include (CLOCKWISE FROM TOP LEFT): Russian sage, black-eyed Susan, cosmos, blue delphinium, sunflowers, a variety of zinnias, ageratum, aster, blue salvia, bachelor's button, scabiosa, quaking grass, larkspur, and blue hydrangea.

As your flower-arranging skills grow, you may be inspired to experiment with different color ways, floral species, and textures. Supplement bouquets with wildflowers or gather blooms from a generous neighbor's yard. A mix of salvia, hydrangea, pachysandra leaves, and zinnia blossoms bloom forth from a vintage parfait glass and look as though they've been hand-painted.

A garden pedestal
or plinth is useful
when arranging to
bring the bouquet
closer to eye level.
A mix of sunflower
varieties is dramatic
when combined with
variegated foliage and
displayed in a 1930's
hand-sponged vase.

Beyond the Vase

Flea markets, auctions, thrift shops, and tag sales are excellent sources for unique vessels that can be used to host floral bouquets. **1.** While it is easy to just grab a vase from the cupboard, floral arrangements will look decidedly more interesting if they peek out from a mid-century sculptural piece of pottery. **2.** A floral bouquet of hydrangea, zinnia, Blue Monday, Salvia, Ageratum, Obedient Plant, and stattice is contained in a miniature cast iron urn. **3.** A clear parfait glass shows off the stems of a delicate-hued bouquet of Hosta blooms, Irish-Eyed Susans, and delphinium. **4.** Asters rest in a bottle-glass dish. **5.** A small blue vase hosts a teddy-bear sunflower. **6.** A single cosmos blossom rests atop a statuette. **7.** Zinnias and long-bristled smart weed fill a vintage collectible.

Green Acres

SEVERAL PASTORAL ACRES ON A HILLSIDE IN NEW HAMPSHIRE BOAST
A NATURAL LANDSCAPE AND GARDENS THAT MAKE A CAPE COD STYLE
HOME LOOK AS THOUGH IT TOO SPRANG FROM THE SOIL.

A vintage birdhouse weathered by the elements nestles into the shade of a Hemlock tree, mimicking the house and its relationship to the grounds.

Prevailing earth tones don't distract from the landscape. Sandy prefers greenery over flowers in her garden beds, and she layers natural elements like stone, wood, metal, and cotton canvas.

160 Matthew Mead

Sandy and Jim Gorman take the phrase "living off the land" quite literally. Their yard is a thoughtfully tended and edited property of trees, shrubs, and gardens that beautifully frame their home. Sandy subscribes to architect Frank Lloyd Wright's theory that a house should fit seamlessly into the landscape. With that in mind Sandy and Jim carefully curated their home and yard, painting their house a single neutral taupe color and surround its edges with green shrubs, such as boxwood trees, Alberta spruce, and creeping English ivy. "Everything is neutral and natural," Sandy says. Stones and rocks make patios and pathways; weathered wood fences and vintage gates make natural borders that blend with the wooded landscape. A patio with wooden lounge chairs and a makeshift fire pit made of a cauldron and an old grate is their evening's getaway. "At the end of a summer day we convene there to read books and enjoy the coolness in the air," she says. "In cooler months we light the fire and have hot chocolate and enjoy the flicker of the fire. Last fall our son was married right here in our back yard."

A stone pathway adjacent to granite edging and a succinct row of boxwood tress is a study in Jim and Sandy's signature style.

ALL IN THE DETAILS

"There are many spots to sit and enjoy," Sandy says of her landscaped property, where she and Jim host gatherings in all seasons. The orderly design of the grounds is punctuated by interesting salvage pieces. CLOCKWISE FROM TOP, LEFT: Stone balustrades decorate the corner of the paver-lined patio, their shapely turnings reminiscent of a formal English garden. Wooden Adirondack chairs make natural places to sit and take in the scenery. Clothespins fill up a weathered bag, a sign of the past Sandy lovingly preserves. A patio fitted with a farm table, benches, and an umbrella is an outdoor room that sees a lot of meals made from the fresh vegetables Sandy grows and cooks. The subtle taupe color palette for the house's wood siding turns it into an interesting textural backdrop for brighter evergreen shades.

On this patio, a side table is fashioned from a tile perched atop a log, and the fire pit is a combination of an iron kettle on an old metal grate.

Vintage copper pans are recycled into window boxes. Sandy uses twigs to support her favorite English ivy, which grows at the windows that overlook her backyard.

PERSONAL TOUCHES

1. Sally believes in displaying the wares of her work in artful ways, including these metal fasteners tucked into a vintage plant pot in the garden shed. **2.** Shy Rabbit Farm is Sandy's name for her few acres of paradise. **3.** Old latches, handles, and hinges were all vintage house parts she finds at flea markets. **4.** Sandy created this garden ornament by placing a rusted metal sphere on a pedestal that came from farm equipment. **5.** Adding a touch of nature to a gardener's utility spot, this found bird's nest perches on the sunny window of the garden shed. **6.** The garden shed worktable organizes things in a natural way but also keeps everything at hand. **7.** Graduated plant pots spring forth supplies and tools used everyday in the garden. **8.** A wicker chair padded with a linen pillow stuffed with buckwheat hull is a still place to enjoy warm afternoons.

How a Garden Grows

Having a strong vision from the outset helped Sandy and Jim achieve their garden's look over time. They collected weathered items from flea markets and reused rocks and old posts from their property. Aiming for a casually wild look, they used regiment, such as stone borders and raised wooden forms, to keep garden beds in check.

Wire mesh dividers (OPPOSITE) are useful for growing creeping squash and cucumber, and they give the garden some interesting height. Orderly rows of lettuce, chard, and garlic become fodder for flavorful meals and flavored vinegars. Old stone posts are appropriately weathered. Melded into planted beds, birdbaths invite feathered visitors. Sandy fashions plant markers from stones glued to twigs. Turn to the next page to see how she does it.

Rustic Labels

Industrious and thrifty, Sandy combines wooden stakes with twine and plant pots to create upcycled plant identifications. Use what you can find around your house or inexpensively at hardware stores and home centers, including clay pots, wooden stakes, and twine. A white paint pen marks the labels and won't wash off in the rain.

1 plant pot

3 wood stakes

2 yards of jute twine

1. Any size and shape of clay flowerpot will work for this project, but a narrower pot will stay placed on the stakes.

2. We like the distinct markings of a white paint pen on the terra cotta color, but you can use any color that reads easily. Metallic gold and pearlescent silver would be an elegant an unexpected choice.

3. Hand-writing the plant names is charming and personal. Remember to turn the pot over before penning the labels.

4. Place the stakes in a teepee shape, and wrap twine around the juncture where the tops of the stakes come together. Tie tightly. Place the stakes in the ground, then top with a overturned pot.

WRITTEN IN STONE

To make the short plant markers that Sally uses in beds of both perennial and annual plants, choose flat stones or pieces of rock. Cut or break several sturdy, straight sticks. They should be at least ½-inch diameter and about 12 inches long to stay rigid and upright when poked into the soil. Write the plant name on the stone with a paint marker, then use all-weather epoxy to attach the stick to the stone.

Sweet BASIL

Tall markers also double as supports for climbing plants, and the labels are easy to read. For shorter labels that tuck into beds and borders, make short stakes (OPPOSITE).

Brushed Up

CHALK PAINT FROM COLOR DESIGNER ANNIE SLOAN PROVIDES
A DURABLE, INDUSTRIAL FINISH TO TRANSFORM REGULAR
FURNITURE PIECES AND RECAST THEM AS OUTDOOR
FURNISHINGS AND ACCESSORIES.

On a pretty patio, a pair of consignment store footstools on casters are ideal perches to set drinks on. Paint colors shown: Emile (OPPOSITE) and Paris Grey (THIS PAGE).

Chalk paint comes in an array of colors. We chose shades of gray and lavender (Henrietta: below, front) inspired by stones and garden flowers. The thick chalky finish coats wood or metal in a strong industrial finish that can withstand the elements.

What if you could recycle almost any everyday furnishing with just a coat of your favorite paint color and use it to add interest to your garden, patio, deck, or porch? Enter the ultra-durable and desirable chalk paint by designer Annie Sloan (AnnieSloan.com), which does just that. "Chalk Paint® is very easy to work with. It very rarely requires any preparation, such as sanding or priming, and can be used indoors or outside, on just about any surface—from wood to metal, and matte plastic to terracotta," explains Annie. "It can revitalize old furniture, walls, ceilings and floors with ease." To show how easy and transformative it truly is, we painted a mix of inexpensive flea market finds (RIGHT) with our favorite colors.

A big salad bowl (BOTTOM LEFT) becomes a pretty planter for cabbage and kale. Picnic in style with a lined basket (BOTTOM RIGHT) painted gray (Paloma).

Chalk paint is not only hardwearing; the colors can be layered to create interesting paint effects—like this rattan serving basket, painted in a soft aged lavender shade. (We used Emile, finished with a wash of Paris Grey.)

A ten dollar demilune table is painted using Paloma and then washed with a light coat of Paris Grey. A textured wallpaper border adds interest to the table and receives the same paint technique. To finish, coat the table with weatherproof urethane for an additional layer of protection.

A vintage wooden trash can is recast as a stunning outdoor planter when primed and coated with paint (Henrietta) inside and out. Drill holes in the bottom of the can and line it with stone; plant with flowering annuals in shades of purple.

Moving Tables

Turn a pair of footstools into ultra-chic moveable coffee tables for your deck or patio.

Furniture pieces

Clean, dry rag

Zinnser® Bulls Eye 123 Primer

Annie Sloan Chalk Paint® (we used Paris Grey and Paloma)

Three paint brushes

Paper towel for blotting

1. Wipe furniture with a clean, dry rag to remove dust and dirt. Cover each furniture piece completely with a coat of primer; let dry thoroughly.

2. Cover with a coat of Paris Grey. For the final coat (we desired a distressed finish), load a paint brush with Paloma and blot excess on paper towel.

3. Lightly brush the paint onto the furniture to cover the surface; use a light hand so that some of the base coat still shows through.

Flower Beds

AN OUTDOOR DAYBED NEEDN'T BE JUST A ROMANTIC NOTION. WITH LUXURIOUS PILLOWS AND A TWIN BED-FRAME, ANY GARDEN NOOK CAN BOAST ONE.

A canvas-covered army basket makes a perfect outdoor coffee table. Add a galvanized tray and a potted planter for an instant perch from which to serve iced tea, and simply remove it when it's time to put your feet up. A mixed planter of annuals is an instant arrangement that can be moved in and out of the sun as needed.

Flowering plants in vintage urns and pots can be moved to follow the sun and alter the landscape depending on what is in bloom. Employ planters of varying heights and sizes to create a natural, seemingly unplanned portable garden.

The Victorians had it right: create a lounge space for the most luxurious kind of sleep, the daytime nap. Plush pillows, soft fabrics—backed up by a gentle, fragrant breeze—all unite in the concept of an open-air day bed. We dressed ours with sumptuous linen sheets, decorative throw cushions, and linen peasant pillows filled with down feathers. Whether put to use as a seating area for hanging out with friends or as a place to stretch out with a good book, a day bed is the perfect place to lounge away an afternoon. Linens and pillows can be removed according to the weather, but when the days are bright and long there is nothing arduous about fluffing up the day bed in preparation for enjoying it. Update the look with current pillow patterns and vintage pieces that can be mixed and matched, and surround the area with flowering planters for a dreamy view.

Add age to any metal item—like the decorative relief found on this day bed (LEFT)—with a rust patina kit from the crafts store. Simply follow the manufacturer's directions and bring distinction to sturdy items that call for the authentic appeal of a vintage piece. Showcase a flowering plant inside a galvanized lantern missing its glass (BELOW).

Embellish a vintage watering can with an antiquing paint technique and a stencil. The great thing about a galvanized can is that it can be put to use as both a vase and a utilitarian tool.

ROSES

"The real beauty of warm weather is free time, no schedule, and a plush open-air place to nap known as the day bed."
–Matthew

Create a secluded backyard retreat with the addition of full length curtains that can be drawn closed to ward off the heat of the afternoon sun and/or afford privacy from neighbors. Search thrift shops and flea markets for cast-off curtains (or fabric to make your own) and sew on ribbon lengths to hang on sturdy rods. Everyone in the family—even this pooch—appreciates the luxury of an outdoor sleeping spot. Whether you plump a chaise, outfit a spacious swing, or unfold a cot, daybeds can be set up and taken down quickly, and you can move them to follow the sun or avoid rain drops.

Rose Pillow

Customize your existing throw pillows by merging and re-purposing items to create something new and uniquely decorative.

Pre-made pillow and pillow case

Burlap rose napkin rings

Safety pins

Scissors

1. Cut off the elastic band from the back of each rose napkin ring.

2. Poke a safety pin through the center of the back of each rose and affix the roses to the pillow in an evenly-spaced row across the center of the pillow.

3. Fluff the roses and pillows and display as a focal point on the day bed.

"I often search out fusion projects at discount and outlet stores. These pillows and napkin rings were both in close-out bins at the same store and were calling out to be paired up. While the two components can be stitched together by hand basting, the safety pins are oh-so-convenient when it comes to laundering or easily changing up the pillows."
—Matthew

Watering Can

Create a beautiful, customized watering can that goes beyond its utilitarian function.

Old galvanized watering can

Copper acrylic paint

Verdigris acrylic paint

Gold acrylic paint

Black acrylic paint

Liner brush

Small paint brush

Steel wool

Stencil, downloaded from HolidayWithMatthewMead.com

X-ACTO® knife

Painter's tape

Sponge

1. Wash and clean the watering can to remove any dirt.

2. Once dry, paint the can with a small paint brush dipped in copper paint.

3. While drying, download the stencil and cut out with an X-ACTO® knife.

4. When can is fully dry, distress the surface with steel wool until you achieve the desired patina.

5. Tape the stencil to the can using painter's tape. With a line brush, apply gold paint to the stencil openings. Let dry and reapply.

6. Once dried, remove the stencil. Use a liner brush loaded with black paint to highlight the characters. Distress the can more if desired by using a small sea sponge to spackle the surface with verdigris paint.

Much of the success of a make-shift space is the use of castoff items recycled into new uses. A glass storage jar holds a refreshing bounty of iced tea.

A lightweight day bed or settee can be moved about the garden to take advantage of warm summer sunlight or dappled shade—which naturally lends itself to more restful naps. Pergolas and covered porches are ideal shady spots to situate a day bed, and the addition of plump pillows practically begs outdoor enthusiasts to stop and rest awhile.

Sandwich Picnic Recipes
(pages 32-41)

PORTOBELLO MUSHROOM SANDWICH

Seven-grain bread

Mayonnaise

Gruyère cheese, sliced

Ripe organic tomatoes, sliced

Fresh avocado, sliced

Basil pesto (homemade is preferable)

Portobello mushrooms, grilled and sliced

Roasted Spanish red peppers from a jar

Curly romaine lettuce

1. Stir together pesto and mayonnaise as desired.

2. To assemble the sandwich, smear pesto mixture on slices of seven-grain bread. Starting on the bottom slice, layer cheese, tomatoes, mushrooms, peppers, avocado, and then romaine leaves. Top with second slide of bread.

CRANBERRY WALNUT TUNA WRAP

apple juice

dried cranberries

all-white albacore tuna

walnuts, roasted and chopped

celery, chopped

pepper

light mayo

baby spinach leaves

12-inch whole-wheat tortilla

1. In a small bowl, combine apple juice and cranberries. Heat for 30 seconds in the microwave, and set aside until the cranberries absorb some juice and plump up, about 30 minutes.

2. Stir together tuna with walnuts, celery, light mayo, and pepper to taste.

3. To assemble the wrap, spread tuna mixture on a layer of spinach leaves in the center of the tortilla. Top with a sprinkling of plumped cranberries. Roll up tortilla, tucking in the edges like a buritto.

MICHAEL'S CRANBERRY CHUTNEY

1 teaspoon ground cinnamon

1 cup white sugar

1 cup water

2½ lbs. fresh cranberries

1¼ cups demerara brown sugar

1½ cups fine ruby port (Dow's vineyard, if available)

1 whole fresh orange rind, julienned

½ teaspoon salt

2 tablespoons chopped crystalized ginger (Chinrose brand, if available)

1 teaspoon ground cloves

¼ cup golden raisins

1. Combine water and white sugar in a small saucepan. Heat over medium heat and stir until sugar dissolves completely. Stir in orange rind pieces, and let simmer over low heat for 30 minutes until rind is soft. Remove rind from syrup mixture with a slotted spoon and set aside.

2. In a medium saucepan, combine remaining eight ingredients, reserving ½ cup of cranberries. Stir in orange rind. Heat over medium heat for 20 minutes until the cranberries have popped. Remove from heat, add reserved cranberries, and stir. Let sit for 15 minutes.

3. Store chutney in a clean glass container in the refrigerator.

Easy Rose Garden Recipes
(pages 128-139)

ROSE WATER SPRITZER

1 tablespoon superfine sugar

¾ teaspoon rose water

2 cups rosé wine, chilled

3 cups seltzer, chilled

1. Combine superfine sugar and rose water in the bottom of glass pitcher, and stir together with a wooden spoon.

2. Add the wine, and stir until the sugar dissolves completely.

3. Add the seltzer and serve immediately. Garnish with fresh, pesticide-free rose petals if desired.

ROSE WATER ICE CREAM

1½   cups fresh raspberries, washed

⅓   cup sugar

3   egg yolks, beaten

½   pint whole milk

¼   teaspoon salt

⅓   cup sugar

1   pint heavy cream

¼   cup rosewater

Blackberries for garnish

1. Combine the raspberries and ⅓ cup sugar in a bowl; mash together with a large fork or the back of a spoon. Store the mixture in the refrigerator.

2. In a small saucepan, stir together the egg yolks, milk, salt and ⅓ cup sugar. Heat over medium heat until just before boiling.

3. Transfer the mixture to a glass bowl over a larger bowl filled with ice to cool immediately. Move to the refrigerator to cool completely, stirring occasionally.

4. Once cooled, stir in the cream, rosewater, and raspberry mixture. Fill an ice cream maker with the mixture, and freeze according to the manufacturer's instructions.

5. Serve when ice cream reaches desired firmness, and garnish with fresh blackberries if desired.

Makes 1 quart ice cream.

MINI ROSE WATER PIES

3   cups peeled, sliced baking apples, such as Granny Smith

⅔   cup sugar

1   tablespoon heavy cream

1   tablespoon rose water

Frozen pastry dough for four 9-inch crusts, thawed

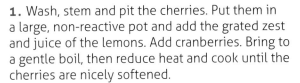

Preheat oven to 350° F.

1. In a large mixing bowl, stir together apples, sugar, cream, and rose water.

2. Line mini pie tins with pastry dough. Fill with apple mixture, and cover with more pastry dough, trimmed to fit. Cut a few small steam vents in the top.

3. Bake for TK minutes.

Makes four mini-pies.

Cherries Jubilee Recipes
(pages 140–149)

FRESH CHERRY JAM

7½   cups fresh cherries

3   lemons

1   cup frozen cranberries

6⅓   cups sugar

½   teaspoon almond extract

1. Wash, stem and pit the cherries. Put them in a large, non-reactive pot and add the grated zest and juice of the lemons. Add cranberries. Bring to a gentle boil, then reduce heat and cook until the cherries are nicely softened.

2. Add the sugar to the mixture, and cook over medium-high heat. Stir constantly to prevent burning. (To reduce scorching danger, you can cook the mixture over low heat, but the quicker you cook the jam, the more fresh fruit flavor it will retain.)

3. There are two ways you can test to see if it's done: Use a candy thermometer and stop cooking when the temperature reaches 220° F (that's the setting point for most jams). Or, put a small white plate in the freezer for a few minutes. Drop a small puddle of jam on the plate and put it back in the freezer for a few minutes. Take it out and nudge it with the tip of your finger; if a few wrinkles form on the jam your finger has pushed, it is set. If not, keep cooking for a bit longer.

4. When the jam is cooked, stir in the almond extract. To store, pour the mixture into sterilized glass jars with tight lids. It will keep in the refrigerator for several weeks.

CHERRY TARTS

1   box refrigerated pie crusts

2   cups fresh cherry jam (see previous recipe)

Preheat oven to 350° F.

1. Spray mini-muffin tin with nonstick cooking spray.

2. Press pieces of dough to fit into each muffin cup. Fill crusts with cherry preserves. Place muffin tin on a cookie sheet, then place in the oven.

3. Bake 30 minutes, until bubbly. Remove tarts with tongs. Cool on a rack.

CHERRY MARGARITA

20   fresh cherries, pitted

3   ounces silver tequila

2   ounces orange liqueur

1   ounce maraschino cherry juice

4   ounces margarita mix

   splash of seltzer water

1. Fill two old-fashioned glasses with ice. Set aside.

2. In a cocktail shaker, muddle the cherries to a pulp. Add tequila, orange liqueur, maraschino juice, margarita mix, and a couple of ice cubes. Shake vigorously for 30 seconds.

3. Strain into the ice-filled glasses and add a splash of seltzer water. Serve garnished with fresh cherries and sage leaves, if desired.

CHERRY ICE CREAM

1   cup heavy whipping cream

½   cup whole milk

2   tablespoons sugar

¼   cup brown sugar

2   egg yolks

½   teaspoon vanilla extract

½   pound fresh cherries, pitted and coarsely chopped

¼   cup semisweet chocolate, coarsely chopped

1. To prepare to make the ice cream base, pour ½ cup cream into a medium heatproof bowl and set it in a larger bowl filled with ice and water to make an ice bath. Place a strainer on top.

2. In a medium saucepan, heat the remaining ½ cup cream, milk, sugars, and salt until sugars dissolved.

3. In a small bowl, whisk the egg yolks. Slowly whisk in some of the warm milk mixture to temper the eggs without cooking them, then pour it all back into the saucepan. Cook over medium heat, stirring constantly, until the mixture thickens and coats the back of a spoon, or, if using a candy thermometer, until the mixture reaches a temperature of 160 to 165° F. Remove from the heat.

4. Pour the cream mixture through the strainer into the reserved cream and stir. Whisk in the vanilla. Let cool in the ice bath until it reaches room temperature. Cover the bowl and refrigerate until cold.

5. Place the custard into an ice cream maker and freeze according to directions. If you don't use an ice cream maker, place the bowl in the freezer, whisking every 30-45 minutes to break up the ice crystals. When the ice cream base is a few minutes away from being completely firm, stir in the whole cherries and chocolate chips.

LATTICE-TOPPED CHERRY PIE

For the crust:

1½   cup whole-wheat pastry flour

1½   cup all-purpose flour

3   tablespoons granulated sugar

1   cup cold unsalted butter, cut into small pieces

⅓   cup ice-cold water

2   egg whites, beaten and mixed with 1 tablespoon water

   Sprinkling of turbinado, demerara, or raw sugar

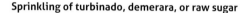

For the filling:

5   cups fresh cherries, pitted

¼   cup dark brown sugar

¼   cup corn starch

   Juice of ½ a lemon

⅛   teaspoon salt

2   Tablespoons quick-cooking tapioca

Preheat oven to 400° F.

1. Combine flours and granulated sugar in a food processor, stand mixer, or large bowl and cut in the butter pieces. When dough starts to form crumbles or a ball, add water and continue mixing until just combined. Finish forming a ball by hand;.

2. Divide dough ball into two pieces, flatten them into discs, and refrigerate for at least a half-hour.

3. Meanwhile, stir all the filling ingredients together in a large mixing bowl.

4. To prepare the pie, roll out one disc of dough, and use it to cover the bottom of a 9-inch pie plate. Pour in the filling. Roll out the second disc of dough. Using a pizza cutter, cut strips in whatever size you desire. Layer on top of the pie in a lattice design, overlapping strips as you work from one corner to the opposite corner.

5. Brush the top crust with egg white mixture, and sprinkle with turbinado sugar.

6. Bake pie for 20 minutes or until crust is nice and brown. Cover pie with tin foil to prevent burning, and continue baking for an additional 40 minutes.

"Roses" watering can pg. 185

ROSES

Butterfly planter pg. 92

Blooming cake stand pg. 112

Essence of the Season

Summer simply isn't summer without the taste of a fresh raspberry. Plucking one carefully off its thorny stem is the best way to savor its sun-warmed juices. But if you pop one into your mouth from a pint box in the grocery store, you're in good company.